New Scandinavian Design

teNeues

Editor in chief: Paco Asensio

Project coordination and text: Anja Llorella Oriol

Art director: Mireia Casanovas Soley

Layout: Emma Termes Parera, Cristina Granero Navarro

Research: Martin Rolshoven

English translation: Scott Klaeger

French translation: Marion Westerhoff

Spanish translation: Almudena Sasiain

Italian translation: Sara Tonelli

Published by teNeues Publishing Group

teNeues Publishing Company
16 West 22nd Street, New York, NY 10010, USA
Tel.: 001-212-627-9090, Fax: 001-212-627-9511

teNeues Book Division
Kaistraße 18, 40221 Düsseldorf, Germany
Tel.: 0049-(0)211-994597-0, Fax: 0049-(0)211-994597-40

teNeues Publishing UK Ltd.
P.O. Box 402, West Byfleet, KT14 7ZF, Great Britain
Tel.: 0044-1932-403509, Fax: 0044-1932-403514

teNeues France S.A.R.L.
4, rue de Valence, 75005 Paris, France
Tel.: 0033-1-55766205, Fax: 0033-1-55766419

teNeues Iberica S.L.
Pso. Juan de la Encina 2-48, Urb. Club de Campo
28700 S.S.R.R., Madrid, Spain
Tel./Fax: 0034-916 595 876

www.teneues.com

ISBN-10: 3-8327-9052-7
ISBN-13: 978-3-8327-9052-3
© 2005 teNeues Verlag GmbH + Co. KG, Kempen

Editorial project: © 2005 LOFT Publications
Via Laietana 32, 4º Of. 92
08003 Barcelona, Spain
Tel.: 0034 932 688 088
Fax: 0034 932 687 073
e-mail: loft@loftpublications.com
www.loftpublications.com

Printed by: Egedsa. Spain

Bibliographic information published by
Die Deutsche Bibliothek.
Die Deutsche Bibliothek lists this publication
in the Deutsche Nationalbibliografie;
detailed bibliographic data is available
in the Internet at http://dnb.ddb.de

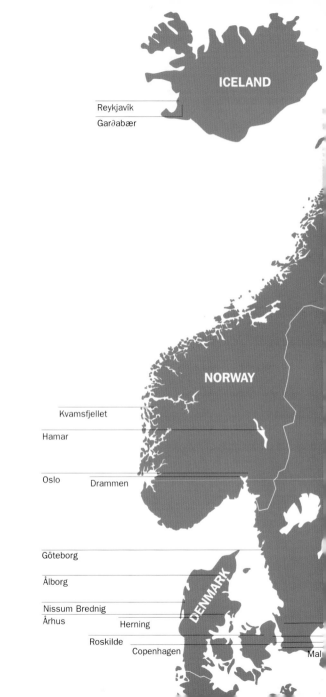

ICELAND

Reykjavík
Garðabær

NORWAY

Kvamsfjellet

Hamar

Oslo   Drammen

Göteborg

Ålborg

Nissum Brednig

Århus   Herning

Roskilde

Copenhagen   Mal

DENMARK

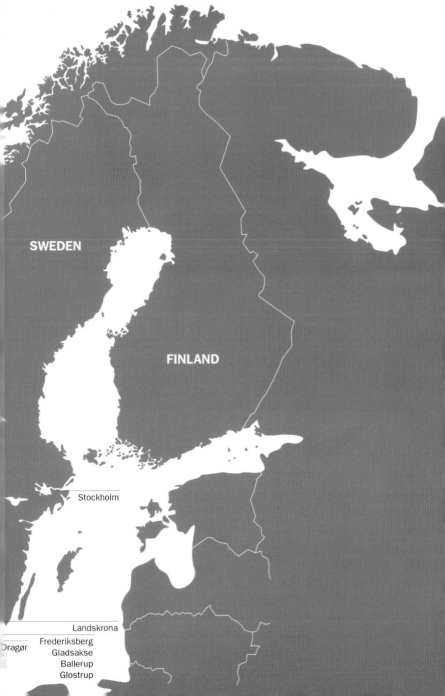

The word "Scandinavian" delineates the northern European countries of Denmark, Finland, Iceland, Norway and Sweden; whereby only the last two actually form the Scandinavian Peninsula. Although Scandinavia encompasses an area of 1,165,000 km^2, which is equivalent to the area of Great Britain, France and Spain combined; only 22 million people live there. Due to the geographic location, the majority of these people live near the coast and in southern areas, where the land is better suited to agriculture.

Besides sharing common historical, cultural and religious roots, the influence of nature and an affinity to nature are also common characteristics of Scandinavian design. The rough climate, nine months of darkness during the winter and bright summers influence the design of interiors. They are characterized by orderliness and austerity. Less furniture creates more space to balance out the lack of light in winter. However, this is far removed from the common perception of a cool, minimalist northern interior and, in fact, Scandinavian design combines functionality with warm and organic materials.

Wood has always played an important role in Scandinavian design and not only because wood is one of the only natural raw materials available. The fact that wood is used so much is based both on its availability and on its insulating attributes. Besides wood, glass and ceramics are also materials used by Scandinavian designers. Innovative glazing, comfortable textile designs, futuristic-looking plastic concepts and bold ornamentation of metal and high-grade steel objects round out the wide spectrum of Scandinavian design, which is rich in ideas.

During the long, hard winters, farmers who often lived far apart from each other were forced to provide for themselves. The necessity to use the raw materials on hand led to an intensive study of their material characteristics. Because industrialization reached this region rather late – compared to countries in western Europe or the USA – high levels of craftsmanship developed.

Nordic design attempts to achieve a balance between form, function, color, texture, durability and cost. Designers like Alvar Aalto, Arne Jacobsen, Jens Quistgaard and Tapio Wirkkala are very nature-oriented. The highest possible simplicity and clear lines, as well as unifying form and function, are combined with organic forms. At the same time, design should be used as a democratic tool for a socially responsible approach, in order to create better products for all people. Despite this long design tradition, Scandinavian designers did not achieve international fame until the 1950s, when an exhibition called "Design in Scandinavia" toured the USA and Canada between 1954 and 1957. Scandinavian architecture did not become important until the beginning of the 20th-Century with industrialization and the growth of urban centers. The Bauhaus movement had a strong influence on Scandinavian architecture in the 1930s. Its stylistic elements were not simply adopted, but were expanded to include human and social components. Buildings were adapted to their surroundings in order to achieve a unity with nature.

While common characteristics of Scandinavian design include an affinity for nature and functionality, design and architecture are nevertheless very strongly influenced by national singularities. These differ-

ences are due to geographic, economic, social and political factors; but also to the temperaments of each individual nationality.

Denmark, due to its strategic location, has always been a link between the European continent, the Scandinavian north and the countries bordering the Baltic Sea. The influence of oriental ceramics and furniture in American Shaker style are examples of Denmark's maritime activities over the years. Danish design has always understood how to combine new ideas and influences with its own culture to create something fresh and new.

Sweden's main economic products were iron and wood, which replaced agriculture in importance at the end of the 19th-Century. For this reason, companies put down roots where they had direct access to forests and hydro-power. Not until the beginning of the 1930s did the population of Swedish cities exceed the number of people living in the country. Initially, urban architecture served only rich citizens in the cities. However, the Swedish government quickly concentrated on improving the living standards of all its citizens. This has lead to new buildings and uniquely high living standards. In fact, half of all buildings were built after the 1960s.

Norway was always known as an exporter of raw materials, a factor that intensified with the growth of the oil industry. For many years, Norwegian products were manufactured without the input of designers. While the Danes, Finns and Swedes were carving out a name for themselves as design nations, Norwegian design lived a rather quiet and secluded existence. Today, however, the situation has changed to

Norway's benefit. The number of Norwegian companies that use professional design techniques in their product development has grown quickly. In 1993, Norsk Form, the Center for Norwegian design, architecture and urban development, was founded as a public institution to advance awareness and understanding of Norwegian design.

Finnish architecture is generally understood to be modern. This is due to the fact that most buildings are new there. Finland did not even begin educating professional architects until the end of the 20th-Century. This lack of an academic tradition, however, has its advantages and Finnish architects are known for their openness and their impartiality. New architectural developments are not blindly adopted, but are adapted to the climate and the difficult environmental conditions in Finland. Saarinen, Aalto and Ruusuvuori are the best known representatives of Finnish architecture.

Iceland is one of the most volcanic areas in the world and is sparsely populated. Many Icelandic designers are influenced by the stark contrasts of Iceland's natural surroundings. This is clearly expressed in their use of unusual textiles and raw materials. It should be no surprise that Icelandic design has earned the reputation of being "somewhat different." Because many raw materials are not available there, Iceland has developed an importance graphic arts tradition.

Unter Skandinavien versteht man gemeinhin die nordischen Länder Dänemark, Finnland, Island, Norwegen und Schweden, wobei sich geografisch betrachtet nur die beiden letzteren auf der Skandinavischen Halbinsel befinden. Obwohl die Fläche Skandinaviens 1.165.000 km² umfasst, was den Ausmaßen von Großbritannien, Frankreich und Spanien zusammen entspricht, leben dort lediglich 22 Millionen Menschen. Die Mehrzahl wohnt aufgrund der geografischen Bedingungen in der Nähe der Küste und den landwirtschaftlich nutzbaren Gebieten des Südens.

Neben den gemeinsamen historischen, kulturellen und religiösen Wurzeln, sind der Einfluss der Natur und die Naturverbundenheit verbindende Charakterzüge des skandinavischen Designs. Das raue Klima, neun Monate Dunkelheit während der Wintermonate und lichtdurchflutete Sommer, beeinflussen die Gestaltung der Innenräume. Diese sind durch Ordnung und Einfachheit gekennzeichnet. Weniger Möbel schaffen Raum, um das fehlende Licht im Winter auszugleichen. Allerdings weit entfernt von der gängigen Vorstellung eines unterkühlt minimalistisch gestalteten nordischen Interieurs, wird Funktionalität mit warmen und organischen Materialien verbunden.

So spielt Holz seit jeher eine besondere Rolle in der skandinavischen Gestaltung, nicht nur weil es zu den wenigen natürlichen Rohstoffen gehört. Seine vielseitige Nutzung basiert sowohl auf seiner Verfügbarkeit, als auch auf seinen dämmenden Eigenschaften. Neben Holz, sind Glas und Keramik weitere Materialen, mit denen sich skandinavische Designer immer wieder neu auseinandersetzen. Innovative Glasuren, behagliches Textildesign, futuristisch anmutende Kunststoff-Entwürfe und die kühnen

Ornamente der Metall- und Edelstahlobjekte runden das breite Spektrum des skandinavischen Ideenreichtums ab.

Aufgrund der langen und harten Winter waren die Bewohner der oft weit auseinander gelegenen Gehöfte dazu gezwungen, sich selbst zu versorgen. Die Notwendigkeit mit den vorhandenen Rohstoffen zu arbeiten, führte zu einem intensiven Studium ihrer Materialeigenschaften. Da die Industrialisierung im Vergleich zu Ländern in Westeuropa oder den USA sehr spät Einzug gehalten hat, konnte die Handwerkskunst ein hohes Niveau erreichen.

Das nordische Design versucht ein Gleichgewicht zwischen Form, Funktion, Farbe, Textur, Beständigkeit und Kosten zu erreichen. Designer wie Alvar Aalto, Arne Jacobsen, Jens Quistgaard und Tapio Wirkkala haben sich dabei stark an der Natur orientiert. Größtmögliche Einfachheit und klare Linien sowie Einheit von Form und Funktion wurden mit einer Leidenschaft für die Erkundung organischer Formen kombiniert. Gleichzeitig sollte das Design als demokratisches Werkzeug für einen sozialen Ansatz genutzt werden, um bessere Produkte zu schaffen. Trotz dieser langen Designtradition erlangte das skandinavische Design erst in den 50er Jahren seinen internationalen Durchbruch. Zu verdanken war dies der Ausstellung „Design in Scandinavia", die zwischen 1954 und 1957 in den USA und Kanada präsentiert wurde. Auch die Architektur gewann erst zu Beginn des 20. Jahrhunderts mit der Industrialisierung und der Expansion der Städte an Bedeutung. So hatte das Bauhaus in den 30er Jahren einen großen Einfluss auf die Architektur. Seine Stilelemente wurden aber nicht einfach nur übernommen, sondern um eine menschliche und soziale Komponente erweitert. Die Gebäude wurden ihrer Umgebung angepasst, um eine Einheit mit der Natur zu erreichen.

Zwar ist die Naturverbundenheit und Zweckmäßigkeit ein dem skandinavischen Design gemeinsamer Charakterzug, trotzdem ist das Design und die Architektur sehr stark von den nationalen Eigenheiten geprägt. Diese Unterschiede begründen sich nicht nur in den geografischen, ökonomischen, sozialen und politischen Gegebenheiten, sondern auch im ureigenen Temperament jedes einzelnen Landes.

Dänemark hat aufgrund seiner strategischen Lage seit jeher als Bindeglied zwischen dem europäischen Festland, dem skandinavischen Norden und den Ostseeanrainern gedient. Der Einfluss orientalischer Keramik und Mobiliar im amerikanischen Shaker Stil sind Beispiele für seine maritimen Handelstätigkeiten. Dabei hat es das dänische Design schon immer verstanden, neue Ideen und Einflüsse mit der eigenen Kultur zu verbinden und etwas Eigenes zu schaffen.

Schwedens fundamentale Wirtschaftszweige waren Eisen und Holz, welche die Landwirtschaft Ende des 19. Jahrhunderts ersetzten. Daher siedelten sich die Unternehmen dort an, wo ein direkter Zugang zu Wald und Wasserkraft bestand. Erst in den 30er Jahren war die Bevölkerungsanzahl in den Städten Schwedens höher als auf dem Lande. Zunächst diente die Städtearchitektur allein den wohlhabenden Bürgern. Jedoch konzentrierte sich die schwedische Regierung rasch auf die Verbesserung der Wohnqualität von allen Bürgern. Dies hat zu einem jungen Baubestand mit einem einzigartigen Wohnstandard geführt. Die Hälfte des Baubestandes wurde erst nach 1960 gebaut.

Norwegen ist vor allem als Rohstoff-Exporteur bekannt, ein Bild, welches durch das Anwachsen der Ölindustrie noch verfestigt wurde. Für viele Jahre wurden bei der Produktentwicklung kaum Designer eingesetzt. Während es den Dänen, Finnen und Schweden gelang, einen guten Ruf

als Design-Nationen zu erlangen, führte das norwegische Design ein eher ruhiges und zurückgezogenes Dasein. Heute jedoch verändert sich die Situation zu Gunsten Norwegens. Die Zahl der norwegischen Unternehmen, die professionelles Fachwissen in punkto Design in ihre Produktentwicklung mit einfließen lassen, ist merklich angestiegen. 1993 wurde Norsk Form, das Zentrum für Norwegisches Design, Architektur und Städtebau gegründet, um als öffentlich finanzierte Stiftung das Bewusstsein und das Verständnis für norwegisches Design zu fördern.

Unter finnischer Architektur versteht man im Allgemeinen moderne Architektur. Dies ergibt sich aus der Tatsache, dass der Baubestand sehr jung ist. Mit der professionellen Ausbildung von Architekten begann man in Finnland erst Ende des 20. Jahrhunderts. Das Fehlen einer akademischen Tradition hatte allerdings auch den Vorteil, dass man in Finnland bereitwillig neue Einflüsse assimilierte. Die Arbeitsweise finnischer Architekten ist durch Offenheit und Unvoreingenommenheit gekennzeichnet. Neue architektonische Entwicklungen werden nicht unbesehen übernommen, sondern für das finnische Klima und die schwierigen Umweltbedingungen adaptiert. Saarinen, Aalto und Ruusuvuori sind die wohl bekanntesten Repräsentanten der finnischen Architektur.

Island ist eines der aktivsten Vulkangebiete der Erde und sehr spärlich besiedelt. Viele isländische Designer lassen sich von den starken Kontrasten in Islands Natur inspirieren. Dies drückt sich unverkennbar in der Verwendung ungewöhnlicher Textilien und Rohmaterialien aus. Daher ist es auch nicht verwunderlich, dass isländisches Design den Ruf des „etwas Anderen" erworben hat. Aufgrund der fehlenden Rohstoffe hat Island auch eine bedeutsame graphische Tradition entwickelt.

La Scandinavie comprend, de manière générale, les pays nordiques, à savoir le Danemark, la Finlande, l'Islande, la Norvège et la Suède. Pourtant sur le plan géographique, seuls les deux derniers se situent sur la péninsule scandinave. Avec une superficie de 1.165.000 km^2, correspondant à la Grande Bretagne, la France et l'Espagne réunies, la Scandinavie ne compte que 22 millions d'habitants. Dû aux conditions géographiques, une grande partie de cette population habite près des côtes et des terres agricoles du sud.

Outre les racines historiques, culturelles et religieuses, l'influence de la nature sur les hommes et leur lien avec elle, caractérisent le design scandinave. La rudesse du climat, les neufs mois d'obscurité de l'hiver et l'été inondé de lumière ont influencé la conception des intérieurs marqués du sceau de l'ordre et de la simplicité. Peu meublé, l'espace laisse la place à la lumière si rare en hiver. Toutefois, il ne faut pas croire que l'architecture d'intérieure nordique, minimaliste, dégage de la froideur : loin de là, la fonctionnalité, conjuguée à des matériaux organiques, rime avec chaleur.

Etant une des rares matières premières naturelles, le bois a toujours joué un rôle particulier dans la conception du design scandinave. Mais là n'est pas la seule raison : en effet, si le bois est utilisé pour son abondance, il l'est aussi pour ses propriétés d'isolation. A côté du bois, le verre et la céramique sont d'autres matériaux qui entrent régulièrement dans les conceptions des designers scandinaves. Émoux innovantes, design textile chaleureux, projets futuristes à base de matières synthétiques et décoration avant-gardiste d'objets en métal ou en acier parachèvent le kaléidoscope des idées scandinaves, aux facettes multiples et variées.

Dû aux longs et durs hivers, les habitants souvent éloignés les uns des autres, sont obligés de subvenir seuls à leur besoin. La nécessité de travailler les matières premières disponibles sur place aboutit à une étude intensive de leurs propriétés. Par rapport à d'autres pays d'Europe de l'Ouest ou aux Etats-Unis, l'apparition tardive de l'industrialisation a permis à l'artisanat d'atteindre un haut niveau de perfection.

Le design nordique essaie de trouver un équilibre entre forme, fonction, couleur et texture, résistance et coût. Les grands noms du design, comme Alvar Aalto, Arne Jacobsen, Jens Quistgaard et Tapio Wirkkala se sont fortement orientés vers la nature. Simplicité maximum et lignes claires ainsi que l'union harmonieuse entre forme et fonction se sont mêlées à l'exploration passionnée des formes organiques. En même temps, le design devenait l'outil démocratique d'une approche sociale, afin de créer de meilleurs produits pour tous. Malgré cette longue tradition du design, ce n'est que dans les années cinquante que le design scandinave fait sa percée sur la scène internationale, grâce à l'exposition « Design in Scandinavia », présentée entre 1954 et 1957 aux Etats-Unis et au Canada. Il faudra attendre le début du 20e siècle pour que l'architecture prenne de l'importance, suite à l'industrialisation et à l'expansion urbaine. En effet, le Bauhaus des années trente a exercé une grande influence sur l'architecture. Ses éléments ont été repris mais aussi agrémentés d'une dimension humaine et sociale et les bâtiments adaptés à l'environnement immédiat dans un souci d'harmonie avec la nature.

La relation étroite entre la nature et l'utilitaire est certes une caractéristique commune au design scandinave, mais l'architecture et le

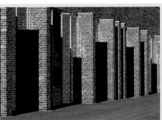

design n'en restent pas moins fortement imprégnés de l'identité nationale de chaque pays. Ces différences ne sont pas uniquement le fruit des données géographiques, économiques, sociales et politiques mais sont également liées au caractère intrinsèque de chacun des pays.

Le Danemark, vu sa situation stratégique, a toujours été le trait d'union entre le continent européen, le Nord scandinave et les pays riverains de la Baltique. L'influence de la céramique orientale et du mobilier de style américain Shaker illustrent bien les activités de commerce maritime de ce pays. Le design danois a toujours su associer les nouvelles idées et influences à sa propre culture pour créer quelque chose d'unique qui le personnalise.

A la fin du 19e siècle, l'acier et le bois, secteurs essentiels de la Suède, remplacent l'agriculture. De ce fait, les entrepreneurs s'installent près d'un accès direct à la forêt et à la force hydraulique. Ce n'est que dans les années trente que la population des villes devient supérieure à celle de la campagne. Au début, l'architecture urbaine est uniquement l'apanage des citoyens aisés. Toutefois, le gouvernement suédois se consacrera très vite à l'amélioration de la qualité de logement de tous les citoyens, créant ainsi un ensemble de constructions récentes dotées d'un niveau d'habitation unique. En effet, la moitié de l'ensemble des bâtiments a été construite après 1960.

La Norvège est surtout connue en tant qu'exportateur de matières premières. Une vision qui s'est ancrée depuis la croissance de l'industrie pétrolière. Pendant de longues années, les designers ne sont pas impliqués dans la conception de produits. Alors que les Danois, les Finlandais et les Suédois acquièrent une grande renommée sur le plan du design, le design norvégien ne fait pas beaucoup parler de lui. Mais de nos jours, la situation a changé au profit des Norvégiens. On assiste à une croissance notable d'entreprises norvégiennes qui font appel aux professionnels du design pour le développement de leur produits. Le « Norsk Form », centre du design norvégien de l'architecture et de l'urbanisme, a été fondé en 1993. Cette fondation reçoit l'aide publique pour favoriser la conscience et la compréhension du design norvégien.

L'architecture finlandaise est en général synonyme d'architecture moderne. Cela vient du fait que, pour l'essentiel, les constructions sont récentes. Car l'enseignement de l'architecture, pour la formation des professionnels, ne commence qu'à la fin du 20e siècle. L'absence d'une tradition académique a eu l'avantage de permettre à la Finlande d'assimiler très vite les nouvelles influences. La méthode de travail des architectes finlandais se caractérise par l'esprit d'ouverture et l'absence d'idées préconçues. En effet, les nouvelles conceptions architecturales ne sont pas purement et simplement reprises, mais elles sont adaptées au climat et aux conditions environnementales difficiles du pays. Saarinen, Aalto et Ruusuvuori sont les grands noms de cette architecture finlandaise.

En Islande, une des régions volcaniques la plus active du monde, la densité de la population est faible. Nombreux sont les designers islandais qui se laissent inspirer par les violents contrastes qu'offre la nature islandaise. Cela se reflète immanquablement dans l'emploi de textiles et de matériaux bruts insolites. Il n'y a donc rien d'étonnant à ce que le design islandais soit connu pour son « originalité ». Du fait de la rareté des matières premières, l'Islande est un pays qui a développé une très importante tradition graphique.

El topónimo Escandinavia alude, por lo general, a los países nórdicos de Dinamarca, Finlandia, Islandia, Noruega y Suecia, aunque desde un estricto punto de vista geográfico sólo los dos últimos forman la península Escandinava. Aunque estos países abarcan una superficie de 1.165.000 km^2, lo que equivale a los territorios de Gran Bretaña, Francia y España juntos, sólo cuentan con 22 millones de habitantes. Debido a las condiciones geográficas, la mayoría de la población habita las tierras costeras y las zonas meridionales explotables desde el punto de vista agrícola.

El diseño escandinavo se caracteriza, además de por ciertas raíces históricas, culturales y religiosas comunes propias, por su estrecha y armónica relación con la naturaleza. Un duro clima, nueve meses de oscuridad durante el invierno y un verano inundado de luz determinan fuertemente la concepción de los espacios interiores escandinavos, que se caracterizan por el orden y la simplicidad. El uso de pocos muebles proporciona amplitud de espacio para compensar la escasez de luz en invierno pero, lejos de la extendida opinión de que los interiores nórdicos tienen un carácter frío y minimalista, destaca en ellos la funcionalidad hecha con materiales cálidos y orgánicos.

Por ello, la madera ha tenido desde siempre un papel especial en la decoración escandinava y no sólo por ser una de las pocas materias primas naturales; a su gran versatilidad de aplicaciones hay que añadir su abundancia en estas tierras y sus excelentes virtudes aislantes. Además de la madera, el cristal y la cerámica son materiales usados e investigados por los diseñadores escandinavos continuamente. Innovadores esmaltes, textiles de agradables dibujos, osados diseños en plástico así como atrevidos ornamentos de metal y acero inoxidable abarcan el amplio espectro de las ideas decorativas escandinavas.

A causa del largo y duro invierno, los habitantes de las aldeas escandinavas, a menudo muy alejadas entre sí, se han visto obligados históricamente a ser capaces de abastecerse por sí mismos. La necesidad de aprovechar las materias primas disponibles condujo a un profundo conocimiento de sus características. Asimismo, debido a que la industrialización arrancó en estas tierras mucho más tarde que en otros países de Europa y Estados Unidos, la artesanía local pudo alcanzar un notable nivel.

El diseño nórdico intenta lograr un equilibrio entre forma, función, color, textura, durabilidad y costes. Creadores como Alvar Aalto, Arne

Jacobsen, Jens Quistgaard y Tapio Wirkkala se han inspirado para su trabajo en la naturaleza. Un gusto marcado por la simplicidad y la claridad de líneas, así como el compromiso entre estética y función se combinaron con la pasión por la investigación de formas orgánicas. Pero además, el diseño se usó como herramienta democrática con una función social: lograr mejores productos para todos. A pesar de esa larga tradición, el diseño escandinavo no logró el reconocimiento internacional hasta la década de los años cincuenta, lo que fue de agradecer, sobre todo, a la exposición "Design in Scandinavia" celebrada en Estados Unidos y Canadá entre 1954 y 1957. Por otro lado, también la arquitectura tuvo que esperar hasta principios del siglo XX para ganar relevancia con la industrialización y la expansión urbana. La Bauhaus ejerció gran influencia en la arquitectura escandinava de los años treinta. Pero ésta no solamente se limitó a adoptar los elementos estilísticos foráneos, sino que les dio una dimensión humana y social. Así, los edificios se adaptaron para lograr la armonía con el entorno natural.

Aunque la sintonía con la naturaleza y la funcionalidad son características decisivas en todo el diseño escandinavo, cada país tiene rasgos pro-
pios fuertemente diferenciados. Las peculiaridades locales no sólo tienen que ver con circunstancias geográficas, económicas, sociales o polí-
ticas, sino también con la idiosincrasia propia de cada nación.

Dinamarca, a causa de su situación estratégica, ha sido siempre tierra
de unión entre el continente europeo, los países nórdicos y los bálticos.
La influencia de la cerámica oriental y el mobiliario en estilo Shaker americano son ejemplos de sus actividades comerciales marítimas. Así, el
diseño danés siempre ha sabido aglutinar nuevas ideas e influencias
con su cultura para lograr en la síntesis una creación propia.

Los sectores económicos suecos tradicionales han sido la explotación
del hierro y la madera, que sustituyeron a la agricultura a finales del siglo
XIX. Por esa razón, la industria se instaló, sobre todo, cerca de los bos-
ques y centrales hidroeléctricas. Sólo en los años treinta, la población
de las ciudades logró superar en número a la del campo. En principio, la
arquitectura estuvo al servicio de burgueses pudientes. Pero pronto, el
gobierno sueco empezó a preocuparse por la mejora de la calidad de la
vivienda de todos los ciudadanos. Ello llevó a un tipo de construcción
muy joven con un estándar extraordinario. Y es que la mitad de los edificios suecos están construidos después de 1960.

Noruega es un país conocido, sobre todo, por sus exportaciones de
materias primas, imagen que fue reforzada aún más por la industria del
petróleo. Durante muchos años apenas había diseñadores implicados
en el desarrollo de productos. En el pasado, daneses, suecos y finlandeses lograban fama internacional con sus creaciones, mientras que el

diseño noruego llevaba una existencia tranquila y discreta. Hoy en día, la situación es más bien favorable a Noruega. El número de empresarios de este país que se vale del conocimiento profesional de diseñadores para la concepción de sus productos ha aumentado considerablemente. En 1993 se fundó el Norsk Form, el centro nacional noruego de diseño, arquitectura y urbanismo, que en su calidad de institución pública tiene el objetivo de fomentar y divulgar el diseño noruego.

La expresión "arquitectura finlandesa" es sinónimo de arquitectura moderna. Eso es debido al hecho de que las construcciones de este país son, en general, muy recientes. La carrera universitaria de Arquitectura no se impartió en Finlandia hasta finales del siglo XX. Sin embargo, la falta de tradición académica tuvo la ventaja de que el país fuera permeable a todo tipo de nuevas influencias. El estilo de los arquitectos finlandeses se caracteriza por su apertura y su falta de prejuicios, lo que no significa que las nuevas evoluciones arquitectónicas se adopten sin más, sino que se adaptan a las extremas condiciones ambientales locales. Saarinen, Aalto y Ruusuvuori son los más conocidos representantes de la arquitectura finlandesa.

Islandia es una de las zonas volcánicas más activas de la Tierra y fue poblada en época tardía. Muchos diseñadores locales se inspiran en los fuertes contrates de la naturaleza islandesa. Ese hecho se plasma claramente en el uso de tejidos poco habituales y materias primas brutas. Así no es de extrañar que el diseño islandés tenga fama de ser diferente. Además, debido a la escasez de materiales, Islandia ha alcanzado una significativa tradición gráfica.

Con il termine Scandinavia si intende solitamente un gruppo di paesi nordici composto da Danimarca, Finlandia, Islanda, Norvegia e Svezia, anche se geograficamente soltanto le ultime due compongono la penisola scandinava. Anche se la superficie della Scandinavia misura ben 1.165.000 km^2, come l'insieme di Gran Bretagna, Francia e Spagna, la popolazione comprende soltanto 22 milioni di persone. A causa delle condizioni geografiche, la maggior parte degli abitanti si trova vicino alla costa o nelle regioni a sud, più adatte all'agricoltura.

Oltre alle radici comuni storiche, culturali e religiose, anche l'influsso della natura e la comunanza con essa caratterizzano marcatamente il design scandinavo. Il clima rigido, con nove mesi di buio durante l'inverno, e l'estate inondata di sole influenzano la disposizione degli spazi interni, caratterizzati da ordine e sobrietà estremi. L'essenzialità nella scelta dei mobili bilancia inoltre la mancanza di luce in inverno. A dispetto dell'idea diffusa sugli interni scandinavi freddi e minimalisti, la funzionalità si coniuga comunque con materiali caldi e organici.

Il legno ricopre da sempre un ruolo fondamentale nell'architettura scandinava, essendo una delle poche materie prime disponibili. Il suo impiego frequente, però, non dipende soltanto dalla facile reperibilità, ma anche dalle sue proprietà isolanti. Accanto al legno, anche il vetro e la ceramica sono due materiali con cui i progettisti scandinavi si confrontano sempre più spesso in maniera diversa. Smalti innovatori, stoffe dai gradevoli arabeschi, arditi disegni in plastica e audaci decorazioni di metallo e acciaio inossidabile arricchiscono l'ampia scelta di idee creative del patrimonio scandinavo.

Nel passato, durante gli inverni lunghi e rigidi, gli abitanti che spesso vivevano in fattorie molto distanti tra loro erano costretti ad organizzarsi in modo autosufficiente. La necessità di lavorare le materie prime disponibili ha portato a uno studio approfondito delle proprietà dei materiali. Dato che l'industrializzazione è arrivata in ritardo rispetto ai paesi dell'Europa Occidentale e agli Stati Uniti, la lavorazione artigianale ha potuto raggiungere un elevato livello qualitativo.

Il design nordico ambisce quindi a raggiungere un equilibrio tra forma, funzione, colore, consistenza, robustezza e costi. Designer come Alvar Aalto, Arne Jacobsen, Jens Quistgaard e Tapio Wirkkala hanno trovato nella natura un'inesauribile fonte di ispirazione. La maggiore semplicità possibile, linee definite e unità tra forma e funzione si fondono con la passione per lo studio delle forme organiche. Allo stesso tempo, il design viene visto come uno strumento democratico con finalità sociali, al fine di creare buoni prodotti accessibili a tutti.

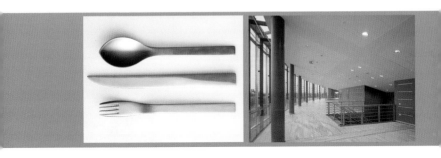

Nonostante la sua lunga tradizione, il design scandinavo ha raggiunto fama internazionale negli anni '50, grazie alla mostra "Design in Scandinavia", presentata tra il 1954 e il 1957 negli Stati Uniti e in Canada. L'architettura acquistò un peso crescente all'inizio del 20 secolo, con l'industrializzazione e l'espansione delle città. Il Bauhaus esercitò un enorme influsso sull'architettura negli anni '30, e i suoi stilemi vennero ampliati di componenti umane e sociali. Gli edifici vennero adattati all'ambiente per creare un tutt'uno con la natura.

Lo stretto rapporto con la natura e la praticità rappresentano un tratto comune del design scandinavo; ciò nonostante, sia il design che l'architettura presentano caratteristiche marcatamente variabili a seconda della nazione. Queste differenze non dipendono soltanto da fattori geografici, economici, sociali e politici, ma anche dal temperamento tipico di ogni paese.

Grazie alla sua posizione strategica, la Danimarca rappresenta da sempre un punto di collegamento tra il continente europeo, il nord della Scandinavia e il Mar Baltico. L'influsso esercitato dalla ceramica orientale e dall'arredamento americano in stile "shaker" costituisce una chiara prova delle sue molteplici attività commerciali. Il design danese, infatti, è sempre riuscito a coniugare idee ed influssi innovativi con la propria cultura per ottenere un risultato originale.

In Svezia, invece, il ferro e il legno rappresentano il fulcro delle attività commerciali, che hanno sostituito l'agricoltura alla fine del 19° secolo. Per questo, le aziende hanno cominciato a sorgere dove c'era un accesso diretto alla foresta e alle centrali idroelettriche.

Soltanto negli anni '30 la popolazione nelle città arrivò a superare quella delle campagne, anche se l'architettura urbana degli esordi era al servizio di pochi borghesi benestanti. Ciò nonostante, il governo svedese si impegnò molto per migliorare velocemente la qualità abitativa di tutti i cittadini creando un nucleo recente di costruzioni con uno standard abitativo unico, la metà del quale venne costruito soltanto dopo il 1960.

La Norvegia è nota soprattutto per l'esportazione di materie prime, un'immagine consolidata in seguito alla crescita dell'industria petrolifera. Per molti anni i designer sono stati ignorati nella fase di sviluppo dei prodotti e il design norvegese è rimasto in una posizione piuttosto defilata, mentre in Danimarca, Finlandia e Svezia esso riuscì ad ottenere una notevole visibilità. Oggi però la situazione comincia ad evolversi a favore della Norvegia; le aziende norvegesi che nello sviluppo dei loro prodotti si avvalgono di esperti nella progettazione e nel design sono in costante aumento. Nel 1993 è stato fondato il Norsk Form, il centro per il Design, l'Architettura e l'Urbanistica Norvegese, per promuovere il design norvegese attraverso una fondazione finanziata con fondi statali.

Il concetto di architettura finlandese corrisponde in generale al concetto di architettura moderna. Le costruzioni sono solitamente molto recenti e la formazione professionale degli architetti in Finlandia ha avuto inizio soltanto alla fine del 20° secolo. La mancanza di una tradizione accademica, però, ha portato ad una assimilazione di nuovi influssi, anche grazie alla modalità di lavoro degli architetti finlandesi, caratterizzata da un'apertura e un'obiettività estreme. Le nuove tendenze architettoniche non vengono acquisite acriticamente, ma adattate al clima locale e alle difficili condizioni ambientali. Saarinen, Aalto e Ruusuvuori sono soltanto i rappresentanti più noti nel ricco panorama dell'architettura finlandese.

L'Islanda è uno dei territori vulcanici più attivi sulla terra, scarsamente popolato. Molti designer islandesi si lasciano ispirare dai forti contrasti naturali della loro terra ed esprimono questo influsso in maniera inconfondibile attraverso l'utilizzo di tessuti e materie prime insoliti. Non deve stupire, quindi, se il design islandese gode della fama di "qualcosa a sé stante". Anche perché, a causa della mancanza di materie prime, l'Islanda ha sviluppato un'eclettica attività grafica di grande importanza.

Residential Architecture

Date : 2003   **Architect:** KHR Arkitekter AS
Address: Tekniberbyen 7, DK 2830 Virum, Denmark
Tel.: +45 82 40 70 00   **Fax:** +45 82 40 70 01
khr@krhras.dk   www.khras.dk
Photos: © Ib Sørensen

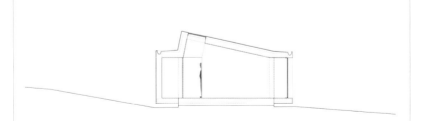

Transverse section

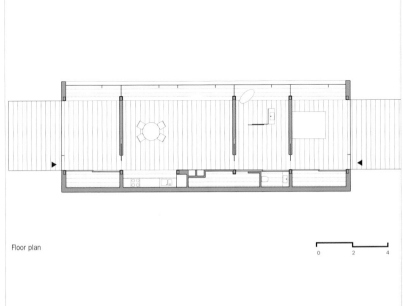

Floor plan

0   2   4

Date : 2004   **Architect:** pk hönnun
Address: Lyngháls 4, 110 Reykjavík, Iceland
Tel.: +354 551 80 50   **Fax:** +354 551 80 77
palmar@pk.is   www.pk.is
Photos: © Åke E:son Lindman

Date : 2005   Architect: LINDVALL A & D
Address: Tågmästargatan 2, 21130 Malmö, Sweden
Tel.: +46 40 30 21 00   Fax: +46 40 24 06 09
info@jonaslindvall.com   www.jonaslindvall.com
Photos: © James Silverman

Axonometric view

Ground floor plan

0   2   4

Date : 2004 **Architect:** Tham Videgård Hansson Arkitekter
Address: Blekingegatan 46, 11662 Stockholm, Sweden
Tel.: +46 87 02 00 46 **Fax:** +46 87 02 00 56
info@tvh.se www.tvh.se
Photos: © Åke E:son Lindman

Date : 2003   **Architect:** Shideh Shaygan

Address: Ostermalmsgatan 52, 11426 Stockholm, Sweden

Tel.: +46 8 23 19 39   **Fax:** +46 8 23 19 39

shidehshaygan@btconnect.com   www.shidehshaygan.com

Photos: © Åke E:son Lindman

Date : 2004   **Architect:** Mats Gustavsson
Address: MGT, Wittstocksgatan 28, 11527 Stockholm, Sweden
Tel.: +46 7 07 17 07 08   **Fax:** +46 86 67 02 31
mats@mgt-int.se
Photos: © Åke E:son Lindman

Date : 2003   **Architect:** Medvind Arkitekter
Address: Holländargatan 29, Box 45442, 10431 Stockholm, Sweden
Tel.: +46 8 30 70 90   **Fax:** +46 8 34 36 50
info@medvind.com   www.medvind.com
Photos: © Åke E:son Lindman

Date: 2004 **Architect:** Arkitektstudio Widjedal Racki Bergerhoff, Natasha Racki and Håkan Widjedal

Address: Hornsgatan 79, 11849 Stockholm, Sweden

Tel.: +46 8 55 69 74 09 **Fax:** +46 8 55 69 74 39

info@wrb.se www.wrb.se

Photos: © Åke E:son Lindman

Date : 2000   **Architect:** Wingårdh Arkitektkontor
Address: Kungsgatan 10 A, 41119 Göteborg, Sweden
Tel.: +46 3 17 43 70 00   **Fax:** +46 3 17 11 98 38
wingardhs@wingardhs.se   www.wingardhs.se
Photos: © Åke E:son Lindman

Date : 2002   **Architect:** SKAARA ARKITEKTER

Address: Drammensveien 130c, 0277 Oslo, Norway

Tel.: +47 22 12 50 60   **Fax:** +47 22 12 50 61

post@skaara.no   www.skaara.no

Photos: © Espen Grønli

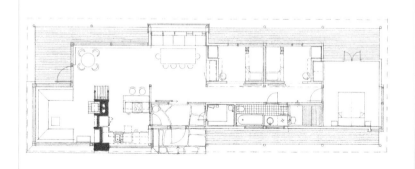

Floor plan

0   2   4

Date : 2004   **Architect:** Meter Arkitektur, Peter Hulting
Address: Koloniagatan 4, 41321 Göteborg, Sweden
Tel.: +46 31 20 43 30   **Fax:** +46 31 20 43 39
info@meterarkitektur.se   www.meterarkitektur.se
Photos: © James Silverman

Commercial Architecture

Date : 2003   **Architect:** Ingibjörg Pálmadóttir
Address: Hverfisgata 10, 101 Reykjavík, Iceland
Tel.: +35 45 80 01 01   **Fax:** +35 45 80 01 00
101hotel@101hotel.is   www.101hotel.is
Photos: © Ari Magg

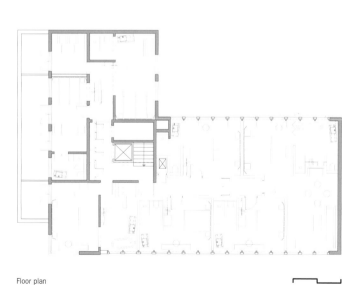

Floor plan

0 2 4

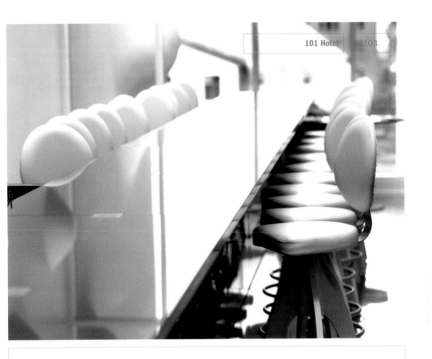

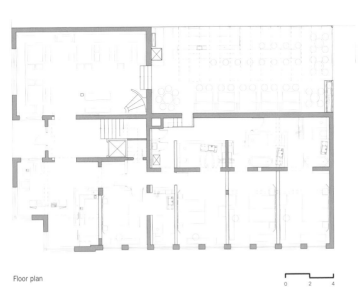

Floor plan

0   2   4

Date : 2003 **Architect:** Scheiwiller Svensson Arkitektkontor

Address: Åsögatan 119, 11624 Stockholm, Sweden

Tel.: +46 8 50 60 16 50 **Fax:** +46 8 50 60 16 70

info@ssark.se www.ssark.se

Photos: © Åke E:son Lindman

Date : 2003   **Architect:** Lomar Arkitekter
Address: Dalagatan 6, 11123 Stockholm, Sweden
Tel.: +46 84 41 77 70   **Fax:** +46 84 11 75 70
kontoret@lomar.se   www.lomar.se
Photos: © Åke E:son Lindman

Date : 2004   **Architect:** Lundgaard & Tranberg Arkitektfirma
Address: Pilestræde 10. 3, 1112 Copenhagen, Denmark
Tel.: +45 33 91 07 17   **Fax:** +45 33 91 07 16
mailbox@lt-ark.dk   www.lt-ark.dk
Photos: © Jens Lindhe, Torben Eskerud

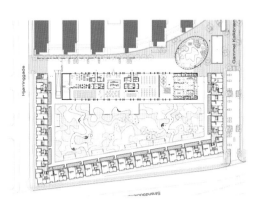

Site plan

Date : 2002   **Architect:** Snøhetta
Address: Skur 39, Vippetangen, 0150 Oslo, Norway
Tel.: +47 24 15 60 60   **Fax:** +47 24 15 60 61
ole@snoarc.no   www.snoarc.no
Photos: © Damian Heinisch

Date : 1999   **Architect:** LINDVALL A & D

Address: Tågmästargatan 2, 21130 Malmö, Sweden

Tel.: +46 40 30 21 00   **Fax:** +46 40 24 06 09

info@jonaslindvall.com   www.jonaslindvall.com

Photos: © Åke E:son Lindman

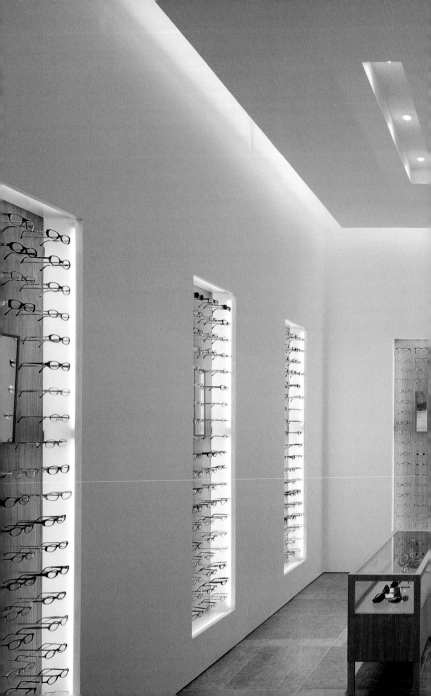

Date : 2004   **Architect:** KHR Arkitekter

Address: Tekniberbyen 7, 2830 Virum, Denmark

Tel.: +45 82 40 70 00   **Fax:** +45 82 40 70 01

khr@khras.dk   www.khras.dk

Photos: © Adam Mørk

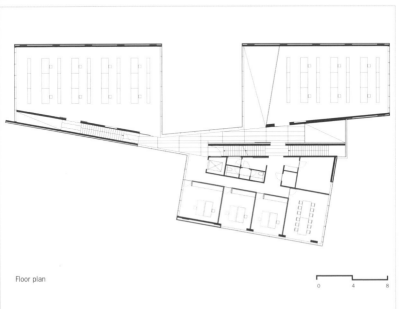

Floor plan

0   4   8

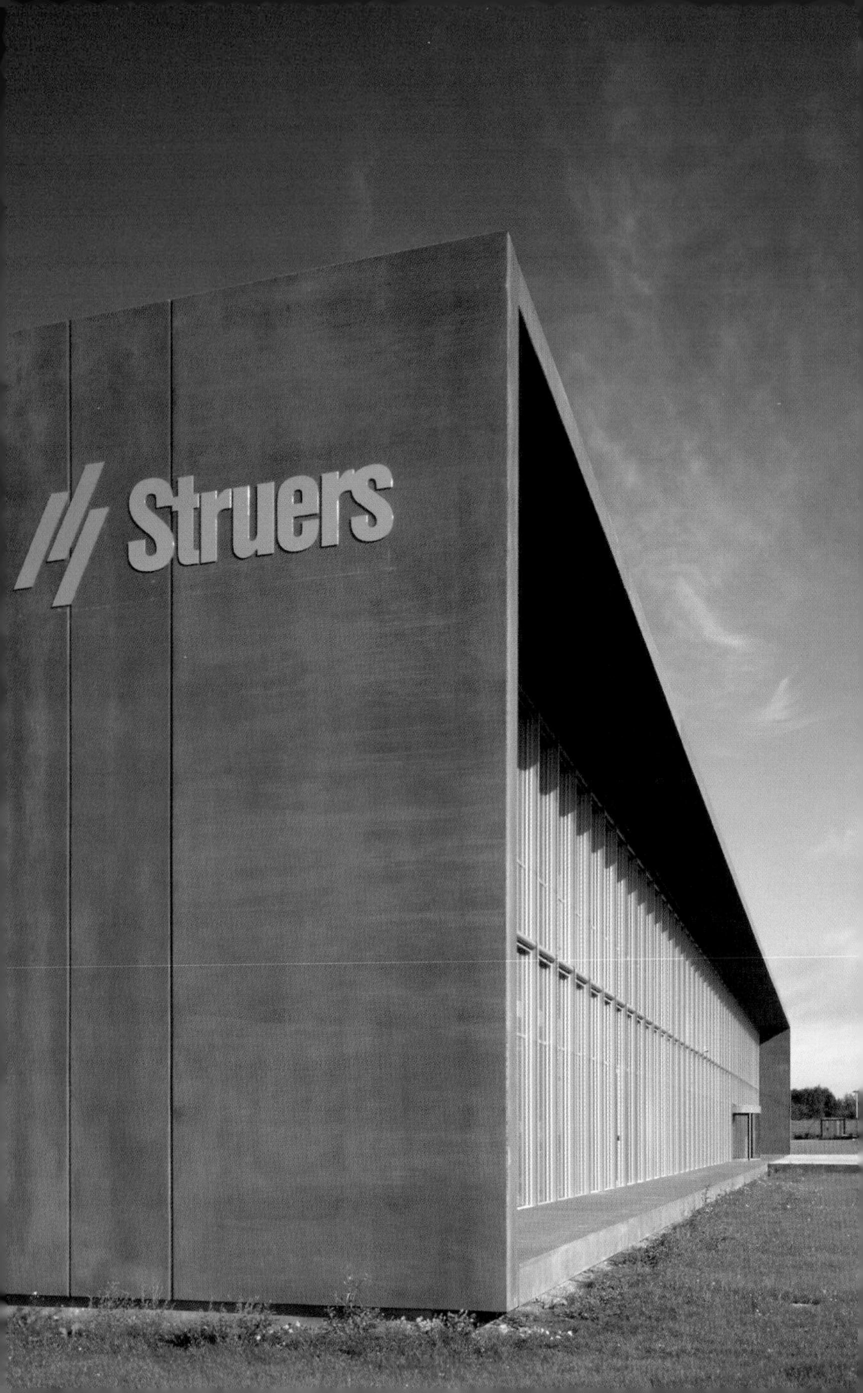
Struers

Date : 2003   Architect: DISSING + WEITLING arkitektfirma
Address: Dronningensgade 68, 1420 Copenhagen, Denmark
Tel.: +45 32 83 50 00   Fax: +45 32 83 51 00
dw@dw.dk   www.dw.dk
Photos: © Adam Mørk

Date : 2001   **Architect:** DISSING + WEITLING arkitektfirma
Address: Dronningensgade 68, 1420 Copenhagen, Denmark
Tel.: +45 32 83 50 00   **Fax:** +45 32 83 51 00
dw@dw.dk   www.dw.dk
Photos: © Adam Mørk

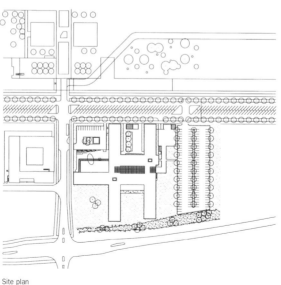

Site plan

Floor plan

0   20   40

Date : 2003   **Architect:** DISSING + WEITLING arkitektfirma
Address: Dronningensgade 68, 1420 Copenhagen, Denmark
Tel.: +45 32 83 50 00   **Fax:** +45 32 83 51 00
dw@dw.dk   www.dw.dk
Photos: © Adam Mørk

Date : 2001   **Architect:** Lundgaard & Tranberg Arkitektfirma

Address: Pilestræde 10. 3, 1112 Copenhagen, Denmark

Tel.: +45 33 91 07 17   **Fax:** +45 33 91 07 16

mailbox@lt-ark.dk   www.lt-ark.dk

Photos: © Jens Lindhe

Date : 2001   **Architect:** SKAARA ARKITEKTER
Address: Drammensveien 130c, 0277 Oslo, Norway
Tel.: +47 22 12 50 60   **Fax:** +47 22 12 50 61
post@skaara.no   www.skaara.no
Photos: © Espen Grønli

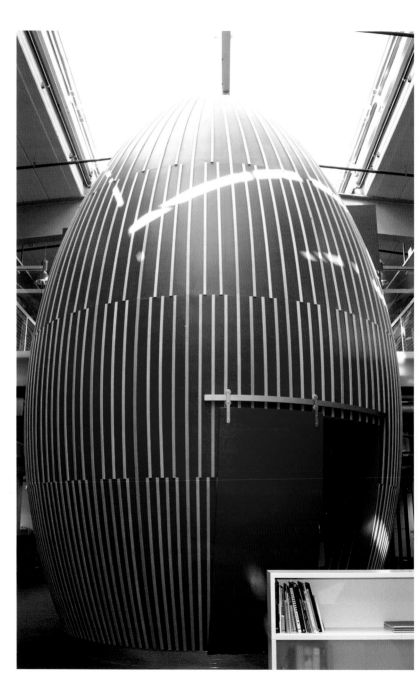

Date: 2001   **Architect:** Kristin Jarmund Arkitekter
Address: Drammensveien 44, 0271 Oslo, Norway
Tel: +47 22 92 60 60   **Fax:** +47 22 92 60 61
firmapost@kjark.no   www.kjark.no
Photos: © Jiri Havran

Axonometric view

Date : 2000   **Architect:** DISSING + WEITLING arkitektfirma
Address: Dronningensgade 68, 1420 Copenhagen, Denmark
Tel.: +45 32 83 50 00   **Fax:** +45 32 83 51 00
dw@dw.dk   www.dw.dk
Photos: © Adam Mørk

Public Architecture

Date : 2001   **Architect:** Snøhetta
Address: Skur 39, Vippetangen, 0150 Oslo, Norway
Tel.: +47 24 15 60 60   **Fax:** +47 24 15 60 61
ole@snoarc.no   www.snoarc.no
Photos: © Damian Heinisch

Date : 2004   **Architect:** DISSING + WEITLING arkitektfirma
Address: Dronningensgade 68, 1420 Copenhagen, Denmark
Tel.: +45 32 83 50 00   **Fax:** +45 32 83 51 00
dw@dw.dk   www.dw.dk
Photos: © DISSING + WEITLING arkitektfirma

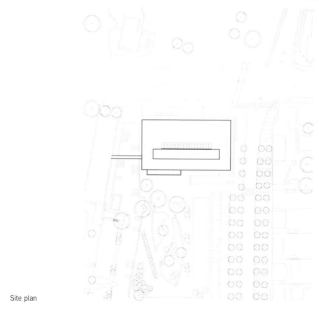

Site plan

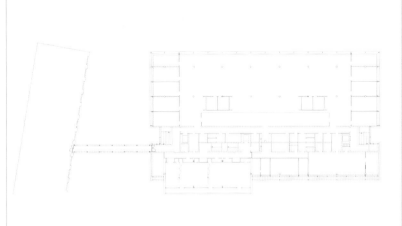

Floor plan

0   20   40

Date : 2001   **Architect:** DISSING + WEITLING arkitektfirma
Address: Dronningensgade 68, 1420 Copenhagen, Denmark
Tel.: +45 32 83 50 00   **Fax:** +45 32 83 51 00
dw@dw.dk   www.dw.dk
Photos: © Adam Mørk

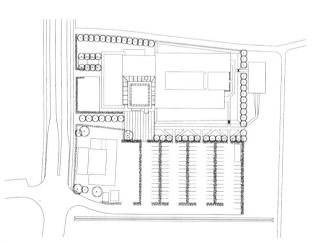

Site plan

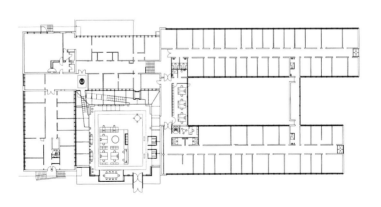

Floor plan

0   4   8

Date : 2000   **Architect:** Studio Granda

Address: Smidjustigur 11b, 101 Reykjavík, Iceland

Tel.: +35 45 62 26 61   **Fax:** +35 45 52 66 26

studiogranda@studiogranda.is   www.studiogranda.is

Photos: © Kristján Petur Gudnason

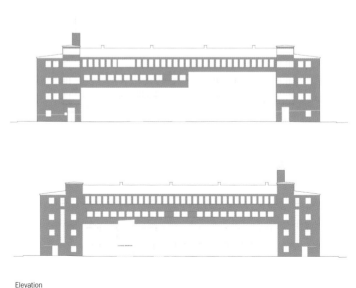

Elevation

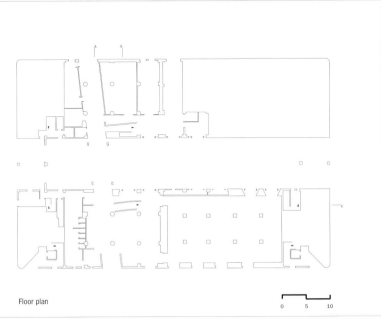

Floor plan

0   5   10

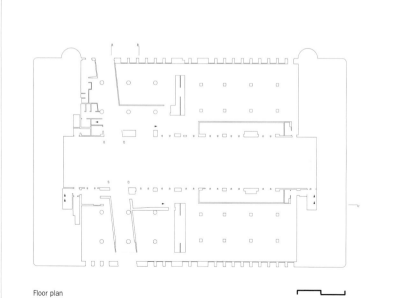

Floor plan

0   5   10

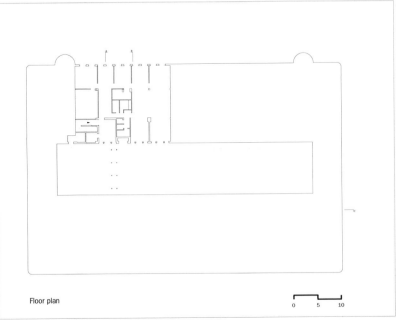

Floor plan

0   5   10

Date : 2000   **Architect:** DISSING + WEITLING arkitektfirma
Address: Dronningensgade 68, 1420 Copenhagen, Denmark
Tel.: +45 32 83 50 00   **Fax:** +45 32 83 51 00
dw@dw.dk   www.dw.dk
Photos: © Adam Mørk

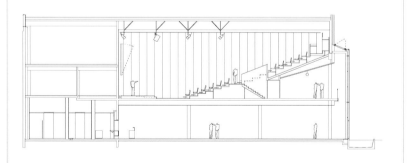

Longitudinal section

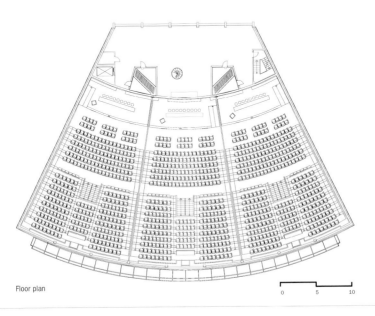

Floor plan

0 5 10

Date : 2004   **Architect:** Studio Daniel Libeskind
Address: 2 Rector Street, NY 10006 New York, USA
Tel.: +1 212 497 91 00   **Fax:** +1 646 452 61 98
info@daniel-libeskind.com   www.daniel-libeskind.com
Photos: © Jan Bitter

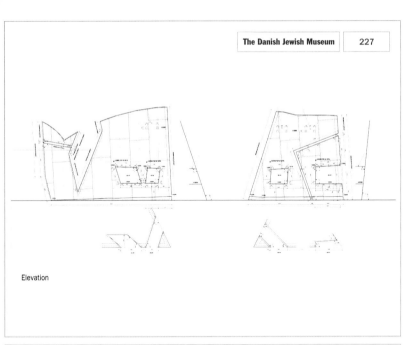

Elevation

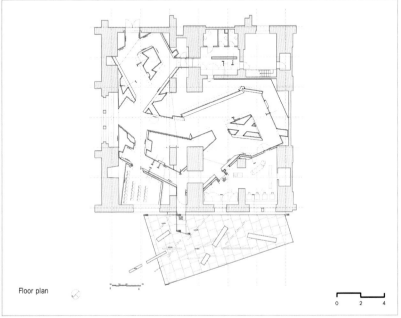

Floor plan

0　2　4

Date : 2004 **Architect:** Lundgaard & Tranberg Arkitektfirma
Address: Pilestræde 10. 3, 1112 Copenhagen, Denmark
Tel.: +45 33 91 07 17 **Fax:** +45 33 91 07 16
mailbox@lt-ark.dk www.lt-ark.dk
Photos: © Jens Lindhe

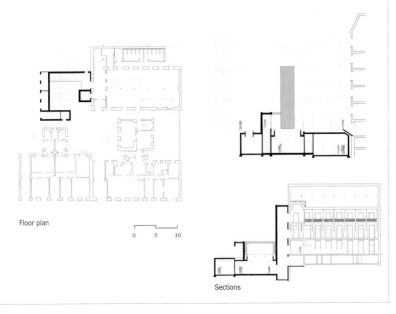

Floor plan

0   5   10

Sections

Date : 2004   **Architect:** Henning Larsen Tegnestue
Address: Vesterbrogade 76, 1620 Copenhagen, Denmark
Tel.: +45 82 33 30 00   **Fax:** +45 82 33 30 99
hlt@hlt.dk   www.hlt.dk
Photos: © Adam Mørk, HLT

Date : 2004   **Architect:** Malmström & Edström Arkitektkontor

Address: Lilla Badhusgatan 4, 41121 Göteborg, Sweden

Tel.: +46 31 13 02 00   **Fax:** +46 31 13 77 00

arkitektkontoret@malmstromedstrom.se   www.malmstromedstrom.se

Photos: © Ulf Celander

Date : 2004   **Architect:** Henning Larsen Tegnestue
Address: Vesterbrogade 76, 1620 Copenhagen, Denmark
Tel.: +45 82 33 30 00   **Fax:** +45 82 33 30 99
hlt@hlt.dk   www.hlt.dk
Photos: © Jens Lindhe, HLT

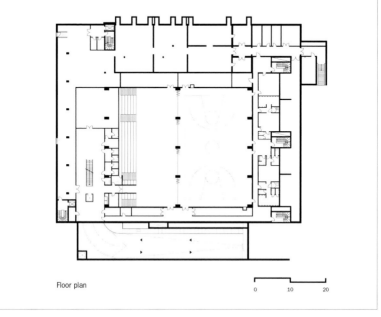

Floor plan

0   10   20

Date : 2004   **Architect:** div. A architects

Address: Industrigaten 54, 0357 Oslo, Norway

Tel.: +47 22 85 38 00   **Fax:** +47 22 85 38 01

firmapost@diva.no   www.diva.no

Photos: © div. A architects, Jiri Havran, Kirstin Bartels

administrasjo

Longitudinal section

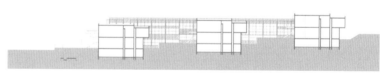

Site plan

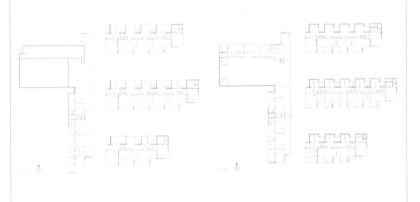

Floor plans

0   10   20

Date: 2003   **Architect:** Kristin Jarmund Arkitekter
Address: Drammensveien 44, 0271 Oslo, Norway
Tel: +47 22 92 60 60   **Fax:** +47 22 92 60 61
firmapost@kjark.no   www.kjark.no
Photos: © Jiri Havran

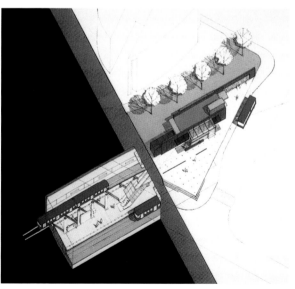

Axonometric view

Date : 2003   **Architect:** KHR Arkitekter
Address: Tekniberbyen 7, 2830 Virum, Denmark
Tel.: +45 82 40 70 00   **Fax:** +45 82 40 70 01
khr@khras.dk   www.khras.dk
Photos: © Adam Mørk

Transversal section

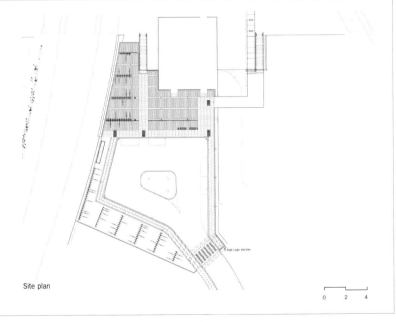

Site plan

0   2   4

Landscape Architecture

Date : 2004   **Architect:** DISSING + WEITLING arkitektfirma

Address: Dronningensgade 68, 1420 Copenhagen, Denmark

Tel.: +45 32 83 50 00   **Fax:** +45 32 83 51 00

dw@dw.dk   www.dw.dk

Photos: © Martin Gruppen

Date : 2004   **Architect:** studio grön arkitekter ab
Address: Kvarngärdesgatan 3C, 1tr, 41273 Göteborg, Sweden
Tel.: +46 31 12 13 71
info@studiogron.se   www.studiogron.se
Photos: © Devegg Ruud

Date : 2003 · **Architect:** Snøhetta
Address: Skur 39, Vippetangen, 0150 Oslo, Norway
Tel.: +47 24 15 60 60 · **Fax:** +47 24 15 60 61
ole@snoarc.no · www.snoarc.no
Photos: © Florence

Date : 2003 **Architect:** Arkitektfirmaet C.F. Møller
Address: Wildersgade 10B, 1408 Copenhagen, Denmark
Tel.: +45 32 64 08 44 **Fax:** +45 32 64 08 99
kbh@cfmoller.com www.cfmoller.com
Photos: © Torben Eskerod

Date : 2003   **Architect:** Arkitektfirmaet C.F. Møller
Address: Wildersgade 10B, 1408 Copenhagen, Denmark
Tel.: +45 32 64 08 44   **Fax:** +45 32 64 08 99
kbh@cfmoller.com   www.cfmoller.com
Photos: © Jan Kofod Winther, Julian Weyer, Arkitektfirmaet C.F. Møller

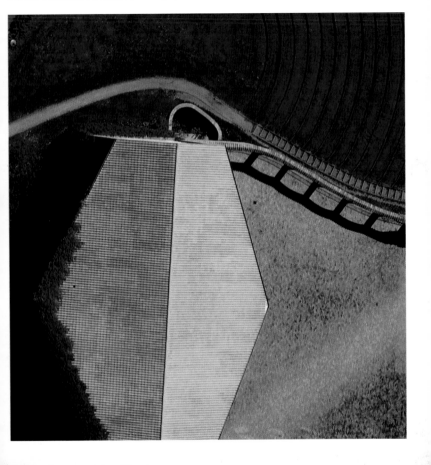

Date : 2003   **Architect:** Arkitektfirmaet C.F. Møller
Address: Wildersgade 10B, 1408 Copenhagen, Denmark
Tel.: +45 32 64 08 44   **Fax:** +45 32 64 08 99
kbh@cfmoller.com   www.cfmoller.com
Photos: © Jan Kofod Winther

Furniture Design

Bird on the rocks *by Ralf Lindberg. 2005*

Bird

Manufacturer: Gärsnäs
Address: Box 26, 27203 Gärsnäs, Sweden
Tel.: +46 41 45 30 00 **Fax:** +46 41 45 06 16
info@garsnas.se   www.garsnas.se
Photos: © Ole Jais

Bird armchair *by Ralf Lindberg. 2005*

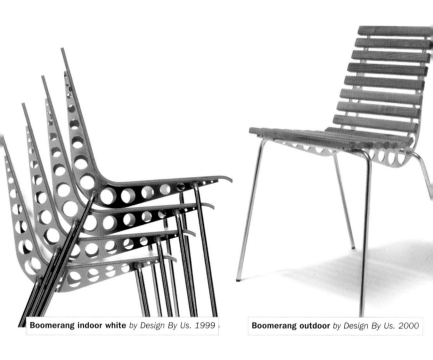

Boomerang indoor white *by Design By Us. 1999*

Boomerang outdoor *by Design By Us. 2000*

Boomerang indoor black *by Design By Us. 1999*

Boomerang indoor walnut *by Design By Us. 1999*

Manufacturer: Design By Us
Address: Rentemestervej 43, 2400 Copenhagen NV, Denmark
Tel.: +45 38 11 80 86 **Fax:** +45 38 11 80 96
mail@design-by-us.com   www.design-by-us.com
Photos: © Strange Photography

Boomerang indoor white *by Design By Us. 1999*

Gubi Stool *by Komplot Design.* 2003

Gubi

Manufacturer: Gubi
Address: Frihavnen, Klubiensvej 7–9, Pakhus 53, 2100 Copenhagen Ø, Denmark
Tel.: +45 33 32 63 68   **Fax:** +45 33 32 60 69
gubi@gubi.dk   www.gubi.dk
Photos: © Thomas Ibsen

Big Gubi by Komplot Design. 2003

Gubi Chair by Komplot Design. 2003

Python by Komplot Design. 2004

Python by Komplot Design. 2004

Python by Komplot Design. 2004

Python by Komplot Design. 2004

Manufacturer: BFDF
Address: Marijas street 13/2, Berga Bazars, 1050 Riga LV, Latvia
Tel.: +37 17 28 92 98   **Fax:** +37 17 24 32 13
bfdf@bfdf.lv   www.bfdf.lv
Photos: © Aigars Altenbergs

Python by Komplot Design. 2004

Ocean chair *by Hans Thyge. 2005*

Ocean

Manufacturer: Trip Trap
Address: Havnevej 11, 9560 Hadsund, Denmark
Tel.: +45 99 52 52 00   **Fax:** +45 99 52 52 29
info@triptrap.dk   www.triptrap.dk
Photos: © Soeren Larsen

Ocean chair and Ocean table *by Hans Thyge. 2005*

Imprint by Johannes Foersom & Peter Hiort-Lorenzen. 2005

Imprint

Manufacturer: Lammhults Möbel

Address: Box 26, Växjövägen 41, 36030 Lammhult, Sweden

Tel.: +46 472 26 95 00 **Fax:** +46 472 26 05 70

info@lammhults.se   www.lammhults.se

Photos: © Piotr & Co. Fotografi Aps

Imprint by Johannes Foersom & Peter Hiort-Lorenzen. 2005

ONO meeting table and SALA Lux chair *by Hans Thyge. 2003*

Manufacturer: R. Randers

Address: Rådhusgade 100, Box 70, 8300 Odder, Denmark

Tel.: +45 87 80 22 22   **Fax:** +45 87 80 22 44

randers@r-randers.dk   www.r-randers.dk

Photos: © Erik Zappon

ONO meeting glass table and SALA chair *by Hans Thyge. 2003*

ONO break café table high *by Hans Thyge. 2003*

Manufacturer: R. Randers

Address: Rådhusgade 100, Box 70, 8300 Odder, Denmark

Tel.: +45 87 80 22 22   **Fax:** +45 87 80 22 44

randers@r-randers.dk   www.r-randers.dk

Photos: © Erik Zappon

ONO break café table and ONO chair *by Hans Thyge. 2003*

ONO meeting table *by Hans Thyge. 2003*

ONO break café table *by Hans Thyge. 2003*

ONO break café table high *by Hans Thyge. 2003*

Spenzer *by Nils-Ole Zib. 2004*

Spenzer

Manufacturer: Källemo
Address: Box 605, 33126 Värnamo, Sweden
Tel.: +46 37 01 50 00 **Fax:** +46 37 01 50 60
info@kallemo.se   www.kallemo.se
Photos: © Källemo

Spenzer by Nils-Ole Zib. 2004

Split table *by Anna von Schewen. 2005*

Split table

Manufacturer: Gärsnäs
Address: Box 26, 27203 Gärsnäs, Sweden
Tel.: +46 41 45 30 00 **Fax:** +46 41 45 06 16
info@garsnas.se   www.garsnas.se
Photos: © Ole Jais

Split table *by Anna von Schewen. 2005*

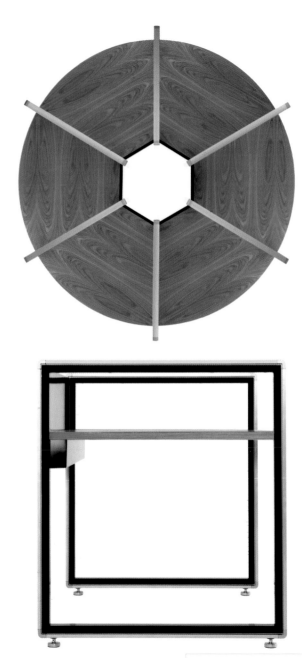

Index Study Table *by Björn Dahlström. 2004*

Manufacturer: Eurobib
Address: Box 150, 22100 Lund, Sweden
Tel.: +46 46 31 18 00 **Fax:** +46 46 32 05 29
eurobib@eurobib.se   www.eurobib.com
Photos: © Claes Westlin

Index Study Table by Björn Dahlström. 2004

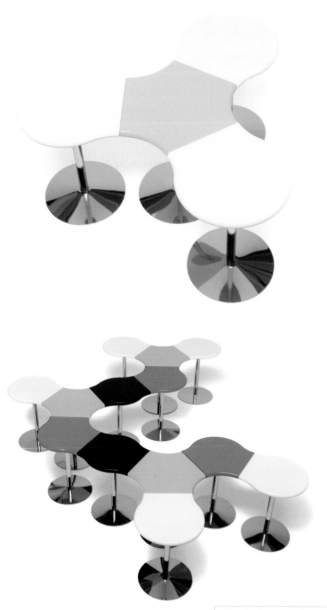

DNA table *by Eero Koivisto. 2003*

DNA

Manufacturer: Offecct
Address: Box 100, 54321 Tibro, Sweden
Tel.: +46 50 44 15 00 **Fax:** +46 50 41 25 24
support@offecct.se   www.offecct.se
Photos: © PeterFotograf

DNA table *by Eero Koivisto. 2003*

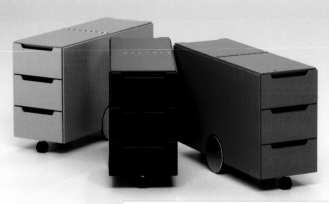

WorX by 3xU arkitektur & design, BERNSEN Enterprise Design,
Duba Møbelindustri. 2004

worX

Manufacturer: Duba Møbelindustri
Address: Vandtårnsvej 62, 2860 Søborg, Denmark
Tel.: +45 70 10 24 10 **Fax:** +45 70 10 24 20
info@duba.dk   www.duba.dk
Photos: © Steen Bjerregaard

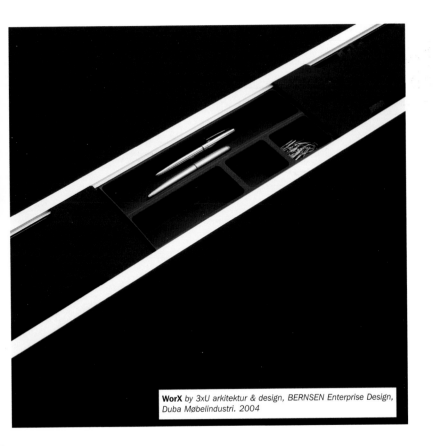

WorX by 3xU arkitektur & design, BERNSEN Enterprise Design, Duba Møbelindustri. 2004

Big Hug *by Anna von Schewen. 2005*

Big Hug

Manufacturer: Gärsnäs
Address: Box 26, 27203 Gärsnäs, Sweden
Tel.: +46 41 45 30 00 **Fax:** +46 41 45 06 16
info@garsnas.se   www.garsnas.se
Photos: © Ole Jais

Big Hug by Anna von Schewen. 2005

Cortina *by Gunilla Allard. 2005*

Cortina

Manufacturer: Lammhults
Address: Box 26, Växjövägen 41, 36030 Lammhult, Sweden
Tel.: +46 472 26 95 00 **Fax:** +46 472 26 05 70
info@lammhults.se www.lammhults.se
Photos: © Studio Wahlgren

Cortina *by Gunilla Allard. 2005*

Cooper by Gunilla Allard. 2003

Cooper

Manufacturer: Lammhults
Address: Box 26, Växjövägen 41, 36030 Lammhult, Sweden
Tel.: +46 472 26 95 00 **Fax:** +46 472 26 05 70
info@lammhults.se   www.lammhults.se
Photos: © Studio Wahlgren

Cooper by Gunilla Allard. 2003

Sunday easy chair *by Love Arbén. 2001*

Sunday

Manufacturer: Lammhults
Address: Box 26, Växjövägen 41, 36030 Lammhult, Sweden
Tel.: +46 472 26 95 00 **Fax:** +46 472 26 05 70
info@lammhults.se www.lammhults.se
Photos: © Studio Wahlgren

Sunday sofa *by Love Arbén. 2001*

UGO *by Norway Says – Anderssen, Engesvik & Voll. 2004*

UGO

Manufacturer: L. K. Hjelle
Address: Box 8, 6239 Sykkylven, Norway
Tel.: +47 70 25 44 00 **Fax:** +47 70 25 44 01
office@hjelle.no   www.hjelle.no
Photos: © Hugo + Åshild

UGO by Norway Says – Anderssen, Engesvik & Voll. 2004

BD:5 easy chair *by Björn Dahlström. 1997*

BD:1 easy chair *by Björn Dahlström. 1994*

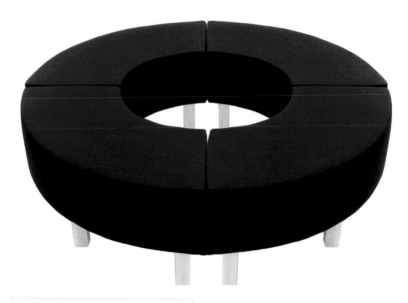

BD:4 curved bench *by Björn Dahlström. 1995*

Manufacturer: David design / cbi
Address: Skeppsbron 3, 21121 Malmö, Sweden
Tel.: +46 40 30 00 00   **Fax:** +46 40 30 00 50
info@daviddesign.se   www.daviddesign.se
Photos: © Jonas Linell and Adam Bankhead

BD:9 sofa *by Björn Dahlström. 1998*

AddOne and AddTwo (without arm) *by Anya Sebton. 2002*

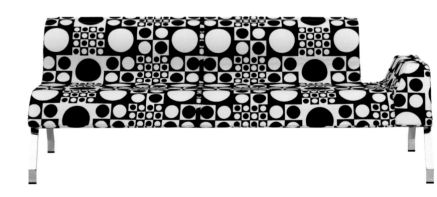

AddOne and AddTwo (without arm) *by Anya Sebton. 2002*

Manufacturer: Lammhults

Address: Box 26, Växjövägen 41, 36030 Lammhult, Sweden

Tel.: +46 472 26 95 00 **Fax:** +46 472 26 05 70

info@lammhults.se   www.lammhults.se

Photos: © Studio Wahlgren

AddOne and AddTwo (without arm) *by Anya Sebton. 2002*

A-Line Modular seating *by Anya Sebton. 2004*

A-Line Modular seating *by Anya Sebton. 2004*

Manufacturer: Lammhults
Address: Box 26, Växjövägen 41, 36030 Lammhult, Sweden
Tel.: +46 472 26 95 00 **Fax:** +46 472 26 05 70
info@lammhults.se   www.lammhults.se
Photos: © Studio Wahlgren

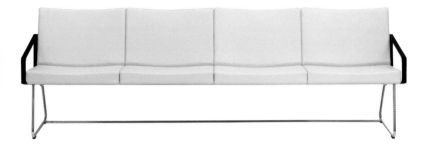

A-Line Modular seating *by Anya Sebton. 2004*

AddOne and AddTwo (without arm) *by Anya Sebton. 2002*

AddOne and AddTwo (without arm) *by Anya Sebton. 2002*

Manufacturer: Lammhults
Address: Box 26, Växjövägen 41, 36030 Lammhult, Sweden
Tel.: +46 472 26 95 00 **Fax:** +46 472 26 05 70
info@lammhults.se   www.lammhults.se
Photos: © Studio Wahlgren

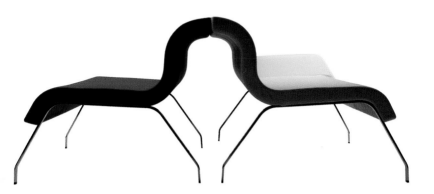

AddOne and AddTwo (without arm) *by Anya Sebton. 2002*

Soft Shaker *by Ditte Hammerstrøm. 2004*

Soft Shaker

Manufacturer: Erik Jørgensen Møbelfabrik
Address: Industrivænget 1, 5700 Svendborg, Denmark
Tel.: +45 62 21 53 00 **Fax:** +45 62 22 90 24
info@erik-joergensen.com   www.erik-joergensen.com
Photos: © A/P/O/G/S//

Soft Shaker by Ditte Hammerstrøm. 2004

Split easy chairs *by Anna von Schewen. 2005*

Quadratus *by Åke Axelsson. 2005*

Manufacturer: Gärsnäs
Address: Box 26, 27203 Gärsnäs, Sweden
Tel.: +46 41 45 30 00 **Fax:** +46 41 45 06 16
info@garsnas.se   www.garsnas.se
Photos: © Ole Jais

Split serie (Split easy chairs with lamp) *by Anna von Schewen. 2005*

Pole light *by Vesa Hinkola, Markus Nevalainen, Rane Vaskivuori. 2002*

Manufacturer: David design
Address: Skeppsbron 3, 21121 Malmö, Sweden
Tel.: +46 40 30 00 00   **Fax:** +46 40 30 00 50
info@daviddesign.se   www.daviddesign.se
Photos: © Adam Bankhead and Anna&Petra

Hanging light by Vesa Hinkola, Markus Nevalainen, Rane Vaskivuori. 2002

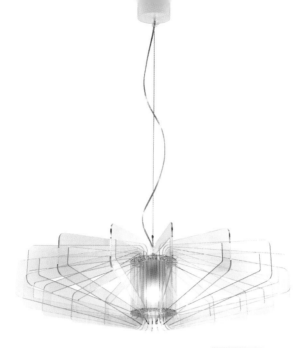

Light Frame *by Stephen Burks. 2003*

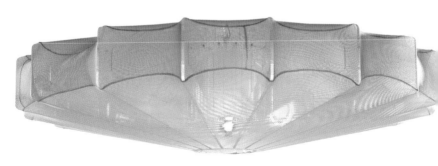

Light Frame *by Stephen Burks. 2003*

Light Frame

Manufacturer: David design
Address: Skeppsbron 3, 21121 Malmö, Sweden
Tel.: +46 40 30 00 00   **Fax:** +46 40 30 00 50
info@daviddesign.se   www.daviddesign.se
Photos: © Adam Bankhead and Anna&Petra

Light Frame by Stephen Burks. 2003

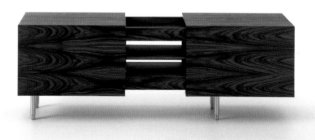

Speyside by Jonas Lindvall. 2003

Speyside by Jonas Lindvall. 2003

Manufacturer: de Nord

Address: Box 229, 20122 Malmö, Sweden

Tel.: +46 40 47 35 75   **Fax:** +46 40 47 35 71

info@denord.com   www.denord.com

Photos: © Johan Kálen

Speyside by Jonas Lindvall. 2003

Product Design

Pipette Glass *by Lovorika Banovic. 2004*

Pipette Glass *by Lovorika Banovic. 2004*

Manufacturer: Menu
Address: Kongevejen 2, 3480 Fredensborg, Denmark
Tel.: +45 48 40 61 00   **Fax:** +45 48 40 61 01
info@menu.as   www.menu.as
Photos: Peter Madsen

Pipette Glass *by Lovorika Banovic. 2004*

LaminaPlusLiber *by Olof Söderholm. 2000*

LaminaPlusLiber *by Olof Söderholm. 2000*

LaminaPlusLiber *by Olof Söderholm. 2000*

Manufacturer: Simplicitas
Address: Grävlingsbacken 2, 13150 Saltsjö-Duvnäs, Sweden
Tel.: +46 86 61 00 91 **Fax:** +46 86 67 37 45
info@simplicitas.se www.simplicitas.se
Photos: Simplicitas

LaminaPlusLiber by Olof Söderholm. 2000

EVA SOLO knife magnets *by Tools Design (Claus Jensen, Henrik Holbæk). 2004*

Eva Solo

Manufacturer: EVA DENMARK
Address: Måløv Teknikerby 18–20, 2760 Måløv, Denmark
Tel.: +45 36 73 20 60   **Fax:** +45 36 70 74 11
mail@evadenmark.com   www.evadenmark.com
Photos: © Tools Design (Claus Jensen, Henrik Holbæk)

EVA SOLO tea maker by Tools Design (Claus Jensen, Henrik Holbæk). 2004

Serving Collection by Lovorika Banovic, Pernille Vea. 2004

Serving Collection by Lovorika Banovic, Pernille Vea. 2004

Manufacturer: Menu
Address: Kongevejen 2, 3480 Fredensborg, Denmark
Tel.: +45 48 40 61 00   **Fax:** +45 48 40 61 01
info@menu.as   www.menu.as
Photos: Peter Madsen

Serving Collection by Lovorika Banovic, Pernille Vea. 2004

Egg by Jens Olav Hetland
(Inhouse Design Figgjo). 2004

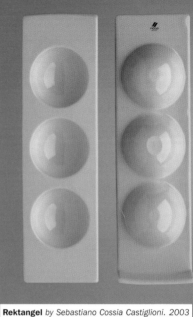

Rektangel by Sebastiano Cossia Castiglioni. 2003

Hval by Olav Joa (Inhouse Design Figgjo). 2003

Hval by Olav Joa (Inhouse Design Figgjo). 2003

Front and Ting series

Manufacturer: Figgjo
Address: Aaslandsbakken 1, 4332 Figgjo, Norway
Tel.: +47 51 68 35 00   **Fax:** +47 51 68 35 01
figgjo@figgjo.no   www.figgjo.com
Photos: Egon Gade

Ting by Ingegerd Råman. 2002

Form Trays by Jens Olav Hetland
(Inhouse Design Figgjo). 2000

Vertica Bar & Wine Set *by DesignIt. 2005*

Vertica Bar & Wine Set *by DesignIt. 2005*

Vertica Bar & Wine Set *by DesignIt. 2005*

Vertica Bar & Wine Set *by DesignIt. 2005*

Vertica Bar & Wine Set

Manufacturer: Georg Jensen
Address: Søndre Fasanvej 7, 2000 Frederiksberg, Denmark
Tel.: +45 38 14 98 98   **Fax:** +45 38 14 99 70
gj@georgjensen.com   www.georgjensen.com
Photos: © Georg Jensen

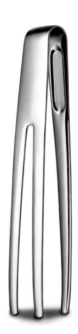

Vertica Bar & Wine Set *by DesignIt. 2005*

Vertica Bar & Wine Set *by DesignIt. 2005*

Jean Nouvel *by Jean Nouvel. 2004*

Jean Nouvel

Manufacturer: Georg Jensen
Address: Søndre Fasanvej 7, 2000 Frederiksberg, Denmark
Tel.: +45 38 14 98 98   **Fax:** +45 38 14 99 70
gj@georgjensen.com   www.georgjensen.com
Photos: © Georg Jensen

Jean Nouvel *by Jean Nouvel. 2004*

Coffee- and Sugardispenser *by Niels Kjeldsen. 2003*

Manufacturer: Rosendahl

Address: Slotsmarken 1, 2970 Hørsholm, Denmark

Tel.: +45 45 88 66 33   **Fax:** +45 45 93 19 99

info@rosendahl.com   www.rosendahl.com

Photos: © Torsten Graae

Coffee- and Sugardispenser by Niels Kjeldsen. 2003

Quack *by Maria Berntsen. 2003*

Manufacturer: Georg Jensen
Address: Søndre Fasanvej 7, 2000 Frederiksberg, Denmark
Tel.: +45 38 14 98 98   **Fax:** +45 38 14 99 70
gj@georgjensen.com   www.georgjensen.com
Photos: © Georg Jensen

Quack *by Maria Berntsen. 2003*

Sakura vase *by Hiromichi Konno. 2005*

Sakura vase

Manufacturer: Georg Jensen
Address: Søndre Fasanvej 7, 2000 Frederiksberg, Denmark
Tel.: +45 38 14 98 98   **Fax:** +45 38 14 99 70
gj@georgjensen.com   www.georgjensen.com
Photos: © Georg Jensen

Sakura vase *by Hiromichi Konno. 2005*

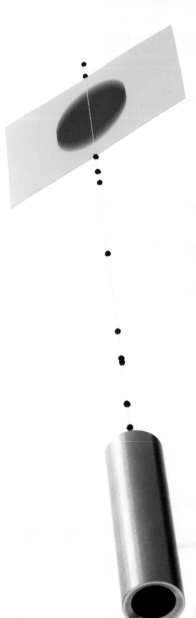

Flag *by Karl-Axel Andersson. 2004*

Manufacturer: Iform
Address: Davidhallsgatan 20, Box 5055, 20071 Malmö, Sweden
Tel.: +46 40 30 36 10   **Fax:** +46 40 30 22 88
info@iform.net   www.iform.net
Photos: © Johan Kalén

Flag *by Karl-Axel Andersson. 2004*

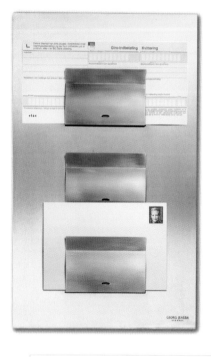

Memory Boards (letter rack) *by DesignIt. 2003*

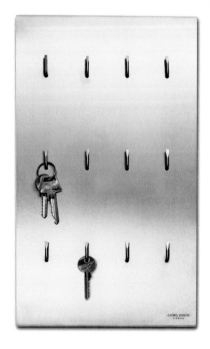

Memory Boards (key rack) *by DesignIt. 2003*

Space Desk Series *by Steve McGugan. 2004*

Manufacturer: Georg Jensen

Address: Søndre Fasanvej 7, 2000 Frederiksberg, Denmark

Tel.: +45 38 14 98 98   **Fax:** +45 38 14 99 70

gj@georgjensen.com   www.georgjensen.com

Photos: © Georg Jensen

Memory Boards (white board) *by DesignIt. 2003*   **Memory Boards (magnetic board)** *by DesignIt. 2003*

Epistola *by Teo Enlund. 1995*

Epistola

Manufacturer: Simplicitas

Address: Grävlingsbacken 2, 13150 Saltsjö-Duvnäs, Sweden

Tel.: +46 86 61 00 91   **Fax:** +46 86 67 37 45

info@simplicitas.se   www.simplicitas.se

Photos: Joakim Bergström

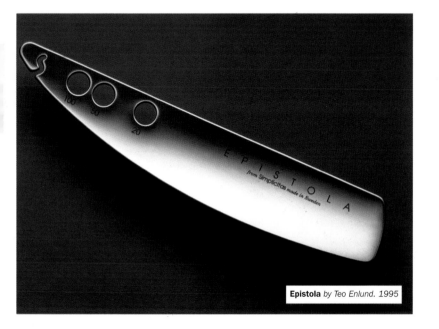

Epistola by Teo Enlund. 1995

Wrist Watch *by Flemming Bo Hansen. 2004*

Manufacturer: Rosendahl
Address: Slotsmarken 1, 2970 Hørsholm, Denmark
Tel.: +45 45 88 66 33   **Fax:** +45 45 93 19 99
info@rosendahl.com   www.rosendahl.com
Photos: © Torsten Graae

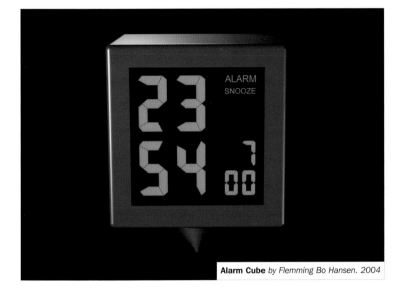

Alarm Cube by Flemming Bo Hansen. 2004

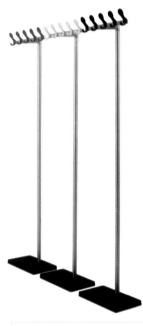

Stand By *by Ruud Ekstrand. 2004*

Stand By *by Ruud Ekstrand. 2004*

Stand By *by Ruud Ekstrand. 2004*

Manufacturer: Lammhults
Address: Box 26, Växjövägen 41, 36030 Lammhult, Sweden
Tel.: +46 472 26 95 00 **Fax:** +46 472 26 05 70
info@lammhults.se   www.lammhults.se
Photos: © Studio Wahlgren

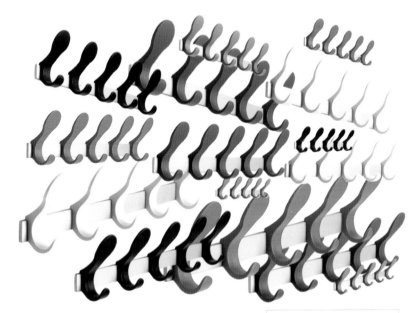

Stand By *by Ruud Ekstrand. 2004*

Info by Ruud Ekstrand, 2004

Manufacturer: Lammhults

Address: Box 26, Växjövägen 41, 36030 Lammhult, Sweden

Tel.: +46 472 26 95 00 **Fax:** +46 472 26 05 70

info@lammhults.se   www.lammhults.se

Photos: © Studio Wahlgren

Info by Ruud Ekstrand. 2004

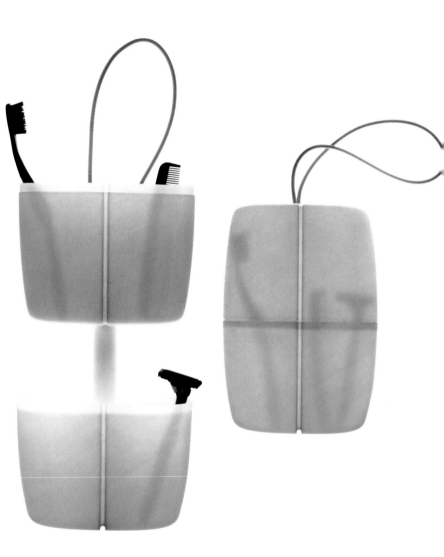

Urbana by Björn Dahlström. 2005

Manufacturer: Simplicitas
Address: Grävlingsbacken 2, 13150 Saltsjö-Duvnäs, Sweden
Tel.: +46 86 61 00 91   **Fax:** +46 86 67 37 45
info@simplicitas.se   www.simplicitas.se
Photos: Mathias Nero

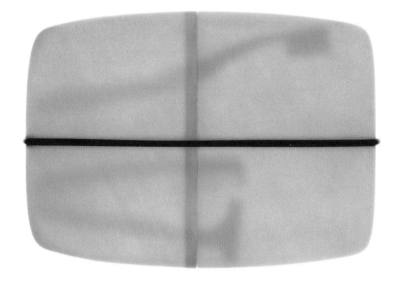

Urbana by Björn Dahlström. 2005

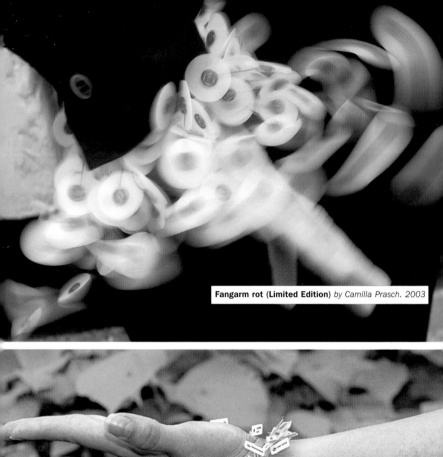

Fangarm rot (Limited Edition) *by Camilla Prasch. 2003*

Registriert Möbel (One of) *by Camilla Prasch. 2002*

Manufacturer: Camilla Prasch
Address: Heinesgade 12, 2200 Copenhagen N, Denmark
camillaprasch@hotmail.com
Photos: Nikolaj Prasch, Dorthe Krogh, Jeppe Gudmundsen Holmgreen

Knotenkette+ schwarz (Limited Edition)
by Camilla Prasch. 2003

Knotenkette papier (Unlimited Edition)
by Camilla Prasch. 2002

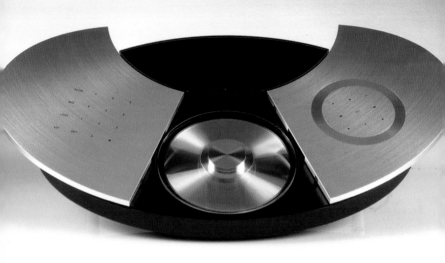

BeoCenter 2 *by David Lewis. 2004*

BeoCenter 2 *by David Lewis. 2004*

BeoCenter 2

Manufacturer: Bang & Olufsen
Address: Peter Bangs Vej 15, Box 40, 7600 Struer, Denmark
Tel.: +45 96 84 11 22   **Fax:** +45 96 84 50 33
Beoinfo1@bang-olufsen.dk   www.bang-olufsen.com
Photos: © Bang & Olufsen MedieCenter

BeoCenter 2 by David Lewis. 2004

BeoVision 7 *by David Lewis. 2004*

BeoVision 7 *by David Lewis. 2004*

Manufacturer: Bang & Olufsen

Address: Peter Bangs Vej 15, Box 40, 7600 Struer, Denmark

Tel.: +45 96 84 11 22   **Fax:** +45 96 84 50 33

Beoinfo1@bang-olufsen.dk   www.bang-olufsen.com

Photos: © Bang & Olufsen MedieCenter

BeoVision 7 *by David Lewis. 2004*

Other Designpocket titles by teNeues

African Interior Design 3-8238-4563-2
Airline Design 3-8327-9055-1
Asian Interior Design 3-8238-4527-6
Bathroom Design 3-8238-4523-3
Beach Hotels 3-8238-4566-7
Berlin Apartments 3-8238-5596-4
Boat Design 3-8327-9054-3
Café & Restaurant Design 3-8327-9017-9
Car Design 3-8238-4561-6
Cool Hotels 3-8238-5556-5
Cool Hotels Africa/Middle East 3-8327-9051-9
Cool Hotels America 3-8238-4565-9
Cool Hotels Asia/Pacific 3-8238-4581-0
Cool Hotels Europe 3-8238-4582-9
Cosmopolitan Hotels 3-8238-4546-2
Country Hotels 3-8238-5574-3
Food Design 3-8327-9053-5
Furniture Design 3-8238-5575-1
Garden Design 3-8238-4524-1
Italian Interior Design 3-8238-5495-X
Kitchen Design 3-8238-4522-5
London Apartments 3-8238-5558-1
Los Angeles Houses 3-8238-5594-8
Miami Houses 3-8238-4545-4
Office Design 3-8238-5578-6
Pool Design 3-8238-4531-4
Product Design 3-8238-5597-2
Rome Houses 3-8238-4564-0
San Francisco Houses 3-8238-4526-8
Ski Hotels 3-8238-4543-8
Spa & Wellness Hotels 3-8238-5595-6
Sport Design 3-8238-4562-4
Staircase Design 3-8238-5572-7
Sydney Houses 3-8238-4525-X
Tropical Houses 3-8238-4544-6

Each volume:
12.5 x 18.5 cm, 5 x 7 in.
400 pages
c. 400 color illustrations